ABOUT THE AUTHO

Patricia (McCormack) Eisenbraun lives in Vista, California, where she can usually be found creating and teaching in her airy, home studio. She enjoys helping her husband, Sam, with his exotic fern nursery, but her true passion is decorative painting. An accomplished portrait artist, Pat first discovered decorative painting over 15 years ago, when she took a group class. Since that time she has created hundreds of hand-decorated items selling some and giving away countless others to appreciative friends and family members. Urged to share her techniques with others, her weekly classes are filled with eager novices, as well as more experienced painters looking to perfect their art. Pat is a member of the Society of Decorative Painters and the Palomar Heritage Painters.

The youngest of 10 children, Pat attributes her love of art to her parents, who inspired her with their own creativity. Today, she is the proud mother of three grown children, Melissa, Matt and Mitch, and four grandchildren, Brandon, Tyler, Matthew and Ashley.

ACKNOWLEDGMENTS

Thanks to Sue Pruett for referring me to Banar Designs. I admire her talent, so to be recommended by her is quite an honor. Thanks to my dear friends Jane, Sharon, Karen, Clara, Dawn, Lori, Claire, Susan, Jan, Debra, Tomiko, and Kayoko, who have always been of great encouragement to me.

DEDICATION

I would like to thank the Lord for bringing this awesome opportunity my way. A friend many years ago said, "God is the talent, I am just the tool." I would like to dedicate this book in memory of my mother, Ethel and father, Henry and also my four brothers and sisters, "Bum," Bill, Betty and Becky, all of whom were creative in their own rights and a wonderful part of my life. I hope I make the rest of my siblings, Nella Mae, Henry, Bob, Jim, and Doc proud of their "baby sister." A tremendous thank you to my husband, Sam, of 42 years, who has encouraged me from the first time I picked up a brush to do a paint-by-number painting. That was it! I started taking classes and have been painting and teaching ever since. Love and thanks for their patience and encouragement to my three adult "children," Melissa, Matt, and Mitch. When someone would ask them if I was busy, I would hear them say "No, Mom isn't busy, she's just painting!"

TABLE OF CONTENTS

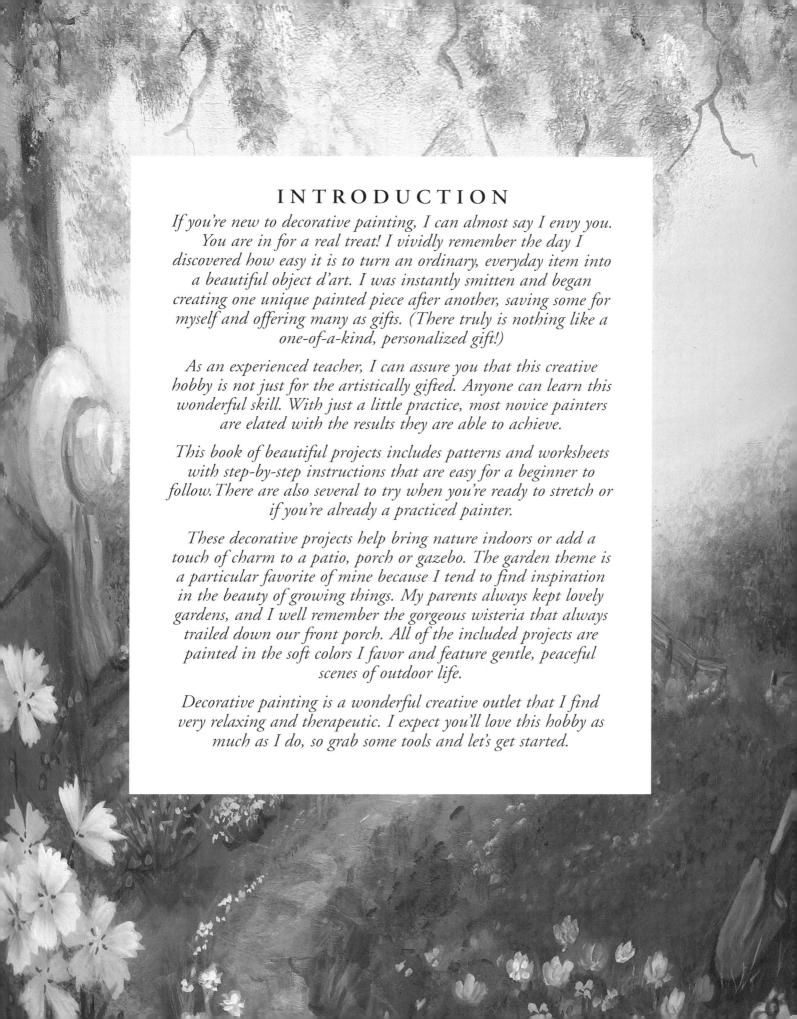

INTRODUCTION

If you're new to decorative painting, I can almost say I envy you. You are in for a real treat! I vividly remember the day I discovered how easy it is to turn an ordinary, everyday item into a beautiful object d'art. I was instantly smitten and began creating one unique painted piece after another, saving some for myself and offering many as gifts. (There truly is nothing like a one-of-a-kind, personalized gift!)

As an experienced teacher, I can assure you that this creative hobby is not just for the artistically gifted. Anyone can learn this wonderful skill. With just a little practice, most novice painters are elated with the results they are able to achieve.

This book of beautiful projects includes patterns and worksheets with step-by-step instructions that are easy for a beginner to follow. There are also several to try when you're ready to stretch or if you're already a practiced painter.

These decorative projects help bring nature indoors or add a touch of charm to a patio, porch or gazebo. The garden theme is a particular favorite of mine because I tend to find inspiration in the beauty of growing things. My parents always kept lovely gardens, and I well remember the gorgeous wisteria that always trailed down our front porch. All of the included projects are painted in the soft colors I favor and feature gentle, peaceful scenes of outdoor life.

Decorative painting is a wonderful creative outlet that I find very relaxing and therapeutic. I expect you'll love this hobby as much as I do, so grab some tools and let's get started.

PAT'S SUPPLY LIST

no. 10/0 liner

no. 0 liner

no. 3 round

no. 10 flat

no. 8 flat

no. 2 filbert

no. 2 flat

no. 6 short flat

no. 4 short flat

no. 8 filbert

no. 8 short round

no. 4 short round

Old worn no. 8 short flat
(Pat's favorite stippler)

Mop brush

Brushes:

I prefer brushes by Royal &
Langnickel. Following are the
brushes I use in this book:
no. 0 liner (2585 Royal Aqualon)
no. 10/0 liner (2585 Royal Aqualon)
no. 3 round (2250 Royal Aqualon)
nos. 4, 8 short rounds (5005
Langnickel Royal Sable)
nos. 2, 8 filberts (2170 Royal
Aqualon)
nos. 2, 8, 10 flats (2150 Royal
Aqualon)
nos. 4, 6 short flats (2150 Royal
Aqualon)
Old worn no. 8 short flat (Pat's
favorite)
1-inch (25mm) mop (1357
Langnickel)
1-inch (25mm) glaze/wash (3070)

Paints

I use Delta Ceramcoat paints because
of their wide array of colors.
Ceramcoat acrylics have a wonderful
consistency and great coverage. But
I've included a conversion chart, in
case you have your own favorite paint.

Palette knife

Palette knives are available either in
plastic or metal. I prefer a palette knife
with a "neck" on it (such as the P-12
from Royal & Langnickel) rather than
the flat style. I use the palette knife to
mix paints and to transfer paints from
one area to another on my palette.

Sanford Sharpie marker

For best results, when tracing your
pattern on acetate, use a Sharpie
marker with an extra fine point
(35000). This marker doesn't smear
like some other permanent pens do.

Sandpaper

Even the best wood pieces need to be
sanded prior to painting. I also sand
metal items.

Dampened cloth

I use a dampened cloth to remove
residue after sanding. I don't use a tack
cloth because it tends to leave a waxy,
oily substance on the object I'm
painting.

Brush basin

This is a container for water that is used for cleaning your brushes. I sometimes use two wash basins when I'm working on a more complex project, one for cleaning the brush and the other filled with clean water, for wetting my brush.

Deli-wrap

I use deli-wrap for my wet palette (see general instructions page 6). I purchase these sandwich wrapping papers by the box at a grocery supply store. If you can't find deli-wrap, you can use a wet palette paper instead.

Water-based varnish

I use a water-based varnish after painting. This protects the piece and gives it a longer life. I usually apply several coats of varnish, letting each coat dry between applications. You can select either a matte, satin or glossy finish.

Metal primer

When I paint on metal surfaces such as tin, I apply a metal primer with even strokes using an old brush. You may need to sand your piece if it's not completely smooth.

Stylus

A stylus is the tool used for applying your traced design to your piece. Most have two size points, one on either end. I also use the stylus to create dot flowers.

Eraser

You'll need a good eraser to remove graphite lines. I use a Magic Rub eraser or polymer eraser, which doesn't disturb my painting.

Cotton swabs

I use cotton swabs for cleaning up imperfections and also for painting things such as wisteria flowers or grapes.

Drying board

Use a drying board to lay down your wet painted or sealed piece to prevent nicks and scrapes. This saves you lots of drying time. I use the Winni Miller Dry-It Board.

Reducing glass

This looks like a magnifying glass, but instead of magnifying what you're looking at, it reduces the image with perfect proportions.

Other Supplies needed:

Delta All-Purpose Sealer (water based)
Delta Metal Primer
Terra-cotta spray sealer
Delta Satin Exterior/Interior Varnish, brush on or spray
Delta Crackle Medium
Delta Texture Builder
Delta Faux Finish Glaze Base
Blue shop towels (from auto parts stores or departments)
Brush cleaner disk
Clear acetate or tracing paper
Draftsman or Scotch Magic Tape
Graphite paper, white and gray
Hydra polyester sponge, $2^{1}/_{2}$" (6.35 cm)
Palette paper, to make wet palette set-up
Pencil and sharpener
Water spray bottle
White vinegar
Chocolate bar
Café Latte

GENERAL INSTRUCTIONS

Before you begin painting, you might want to paint some practice strokes on a piece of paper. This will familiarize you with the brushes, the paint, and also other techniques such as sideloading and washing.

To load your brush, do not scoop up a lot of paint. Pick up some paint on the brush and work it into both sides, blending on the palette until the paint is evenly distributed through the bristles.

Now you're ready to begin. Follow the instructions for your design and the color recommendations listed. If you make a mistake, use a cotton swab to correct the error.

Begin by preparing your piece. If it's a wooden item, sand until the wood is smooth. Remove excess dust with a dampened cloth. Apply wood sealer to close the pores of the wood.

If it's a metal item, sand lightly. (I place the item in my sink and wash it with an old cloth and soapy water.) Then rinse the item with white vinegar. This removes any oily areas. Apply metal primer using an old brush.

Basecoating

Basecoat the piece by applying a solid layer of color until the desired opacity is achieved. You may choose to basecoat the entire piece or just certain design elements.

Transferring your design

I use clear acetate and a Sharpie pen to trace patterns. Lay the acetate over the pattern and trace it. Then place the acetate over the graphite paper (either white or gray) graphite-side down on the object you'll be painting and tape lightly to secure. Go over your traced pattern with a stylus, tracing over the lines (you will transfer the pattern in stages: first, after the background is painted and dried, then forward items as needed). Use light pressure, you don't want your lines to be too dark or your paint won't cover. Check your lines as you're tracing to make any adjustments.

Setting up a wet palette

Lay a dampened blue towel on top of the palette paper, with about a 2" (5.08 cm) excess hanging over one side. Lay a piece of deli-wrap on top of the blue towels. Fold the excess towel edge over the deli-wrap at the top. Place your paints on the folded-over area. If there is extra deli paper at the bottom end, just tuck it under the blue towel or cut it off. The paints will stay pliable longer than on regular palette paper. Always cover the paints when not in use (with tin foil or a styrofoam plate, for instance).

Caring for brushes

When you purchase a new brush, you should remove the sizing first by rubbing the hairs between your fingers, then clean the brush in water.

After you finish painting, wash the brush using a brush cleaner. There are several good ones on the market. Apply the cleaner to the bristles and work it in with your fingers. Rinse with water. Dry the bristles on a paper towel or soft cloth and reshape the bristles.

I use a brush cleaner disk with the brush cleaner. Brush the ferrule, or metal part, of your brush one way over the disk, not the tips of bristles. Repeat several times until the brush is completely cleaned.

When using a brush basin, don't brush the tips of the bristles against the ridges at the bottom of the basin. I swish the brush in the water, then clean the ferrule part of the brush against one ridge.

Never let paint dry in your brush and never let brushes soak in water.

I always put an old towel under my work area. After I wash my brushes in the basin, I lay them on the towel to soak up the excess water.

Mixing colors

When you're instructed to mix colors, it will be indicated with a "+, " for instance, Straw + White. This would mean an equal part of each color. When the proportions are different it will be indicated, such as 2:1, which means 2 parts of the first color and 1 part of the next.

Glazing

A thin wash of paint used to brush over a previously painted surface to achieve a subtle transparent effect.

BRUSHSTROKES

Side Loading

1. Dampen brush in water. Blot excess. Dip one corner of brush in paint.

2. Blend brush a few times on palette. Paint will spread across brush, fading to clear water on opposite side.

Double Loading

1. Dip flat brush in water, blot, touch one corner of brush in paint. Turn over and touch opposite corner in another color.

2. Stroke brush on palette to blend colors at center of brush. Pure colors will remain on each corner.

Comma Stroke

1. Touch tip of loaded round brush down and apply pressure until bristles fan out.

2. Pull brush toward you as you begin to lift to the point (curving as you pull). End on tip of brush to create thin tail of stroke.

Slip-Slap

1. Using a flat brush, make loose x's in a slip-slap motion, filling in a desired area.

2. Continue slip-slapping over the top of the previous x's to build up light and dark areas. Use this technique to make bushes and trees.

Side loaded Chisel

Side load flat brush. Wiggle the brush as you stroke to give the appearance of shingles, lace or foliage.

Side loaded Float

Dip flat brush in water, then side load with paint. Blend on palette. Use for subtle shading or background areas.

Chisel

1. Set chisel edge of brush on surface, holding handle straight up and down. Stroke from side to side creating straight lines.

2. Use the chisel edge of the brush to make straight lines for ferns. The chisel can also be used for shading and texturing.

BRUSHSTROKES

Stippling

Using an old worn brush (this is a short round), load with paint and pounce straight up and down on surface.

Pat Blend

Load brush with paint (using a short round brush) and basecoat in an area. While it is still wet, apply lighter value. Wipe off excess paint and softly blend values together.

Linework

Load a liner brush with paint thinned to the consistency of ink. Keep brush on its tip as you paint. Loosely balance on little finger, using long, loose strokes.

Zigzag

Double load a flat brush. With all bristles touching, begin zigzagging in a half circle. Inside of brush is always pointed to the center. Use for bushes, trees or other foliage.

Pat's "Foliage" Stroke

1. Double load an old worn no. 8 flat brush or "stipple" brush. Pounce brush up and down in a half-circular motion.

2. Continue pouncing, overlapping your previous strokes and keeping the light paint at the top. This works well for foliage and grass.

S-Stroke

1. Set tip of round brush on surface with brush handle straight up. Pull a fine line toward you. Apply pressure, letting bristles flatten out.

2. After applying pressure, pull up to a fine chisel. Pull toward you creating a fine line tail. This can be done in either direction.

Pat's Stems and Leaves

1. Load a no. 3 round brush with paint. Apply pressure, letting bristles fan out.

2. Pull up to the chisel point making the leaf as thick or as long as you want.

3. If desired, pull back toward you to create end of leaf, or just keep creating several leaf strokes. These make nice small tulip or daffodil leaves.

BLOSSOM BORDER

Though this pot is easy to decorate, friends will be thrilled with the hand-painted gift! A terra-cotta pot is a decorative painter's best friend because it's inexpensive and easy to decorate with a simple design. A beginner can create a very simple accent, while someone more experienced can embellish to her heart's content.

This rim design features two easy flowers on a solid background, interspersed with small leaves. Stippled accents of lilac are also added to create luminosity and depth.

Supplies:

Terra-cotta pot
Terra-cotta spray sealer
Delta Exterior/Interior Varnish
Brushes:
no. 10/0 liner
no. 3 round
no. 8 short round
no. 8 filbert
no. 8 flat
1-inch (25mm) sponge brush

Prep: Spray with terra-cotta spray sealer to allow paint to adhere. Base rim of pot with Black Green using a 1-inch (25mm) sponge brush.
Apply the pattern from page 12 with transfer paper and a stylus. Follow the instructions for painting the flowers on page 11.
Spray with Delta Exterior/Interior Varnish following directions on can.

Pale Lilac

Purple Smoke

Black Green

Bridgeport Grey

Chamomile

Woodland Night Green

PRETTY PAIR

When you see what you can do with terra-cotta saucers, you'll never look at these objects the same way again. Once the center is painted, the saucer rim becomes an etched frame for your lovely still life! These designs feature the same colors and flowers as the terra-cotta pot pictured on page 9. More detailed foliage is included here as well as additional stippling and shading.

This makes a set of eye-catching wall plaques, and would look especially pretty with the matching pot placed on a table just below.

Supplies:
Terra-cotta saucer (oval shape)
Terra-cotta spray sealer
Delta Exterior/Interior Varnish

Brushes:
no. 10/0 liner
no. 3 round
no. 8 short round

no. 8 filbert
no. 8 flat
1-inch (25mm) wash brush

Raw Linen

Light Foliage Green

Medium Foliage Green

Dark Foliage Green

Magnolia White

Dark Goldenrod

Georgia Clay

Eggplant

Bungalow Blue

Prep: Spray with terra-cotta sealer.

Backgrounds: Use a 1-inch (25mm) wash brush to basecoat background Black Green + Woodland Night Green. Use a no. 8 short round and Georgia Clay and Dark Goldenrod to stipple at bottom, blending into the background. Let dry. Trace on pattern with white graphite and a stylus. (Use a chalk pencil if graphite won't adhere to surface.)

White flowers: Use a no. 8 filbert and Raw Linen to base flowers and buds. Shade under top petals with Bridgeport Grey.

Centers: Use a no. 8 short round and Dark Foliage Green to dab into center nearest the front petal. Highlight with Light Foliage Green, dabbing into the Dark Foliage Green and blending out onto the petal.

Pollen: Use a no. 10/0 liner and Chamomile to create several dots.

Leaves: Paint comma strokes using a no. 8 filbert and Medium Foliage Green. Shade with Dark Foliage Green. Highlight with Light Foliage Green + Chamomile. Use Medium Foliage Green for the stem, sliding the chisel edge of the brush down.

Purple puffs: Stipple using a no. 3 round with Eggplant and highlight with Pale Lilac.

Violas: With a no. 8 filbert, base petals using Bungalow Blue. To create separations between petals, shade with Purple Smoke. Side load the brush with Bungalow Blue + Magnolia White to highlight along the edges of the petals. Pat lightly with the edge of the brush at the curve of petals as pictured. Use a no. 10/0 liner and thinned Magnolia White to pull fine lines shaped to a "V" on face petal (see below).

Pollen: Use Georgia Clay and no. 3 round to dab in center. Highlight with dabs of Georgia Clay + Magnolia White also shaped to a "V."

Stems: Paint stems Dark Foliage Green with chisel end of a no. 8 flat brush.

Leaves: Double load a no. 8 filbert brush with Dark Foliage Green and Light Foliage Green and paint the leaves. Paint back leaves first. Reinforce stems if needed.

Spray with Delta Exterior/Interior Varnish following the manufacturer's instructions.

Patterns for Pretty Pair

**Pattern for
Blossom Border**

TOOLS OF THE TRADE

A rusty shovel and pitchfork are useful, but decorative? This painted duo certainly is! Both wooden handles are coated with matching Stonewedge Green, so they make a delightful display set. These "tools" could be propped on a hearth or in any corner, or hung on a wall. Add a protective coating and they can also decorate an outdoor fence or shed.

Bridgeport Grey

 Burnt Umber

 Cape Cod Blue

 Charcoal

 Lichen Grey

 Lavender Lace

 Dark Foliage Green

 Deep Lilac

 Old Parchment

White

 Stonewedge Green

 Straw

 Nightfall Blue

GARDEN PITCHFORK

On the pitchfork, dried bouquets meander down the center prongs, anchored by a rustic, green pegboard. This simple design is an excellent one for beginners to try.

Supplies:

Decorative rusty pitchfork
Delta Metal Primer
Delta Exterior/Interior Varnish
Brushes:
no. 0 liner
no. 3 round
nos. 8, 10 flats
1-inch (25mm) wash brush

Prep: Sand handle, then using the wash brush, paint it using Stonewedge Green + a touch of Bridgeport Grey.

Metal: Sand, wipe clean, wash with soap and water, then rinse with vinegar. Let dry. Apply Delta Metal Primer with a 1-inch (25mm) wash brush, following instructions on the label. Sand lightly.

Apply pattern with white graphite paper and stylus.

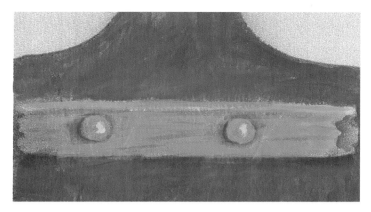

Pegboard: Base with a no. 10 flat brush and a mix of Cape Cod Blue + Stonewedge Green + a touch of Bridgeport Grey. Use a no. 8 flat brush and Nightfall Blue to shade around the pegs and raw edges. Create grain of wood with the chisel edge of brush. Use base mix + Lavender Lace for the upper edge showing the thickness of the board. Highlight pegs with Lavender Lace.

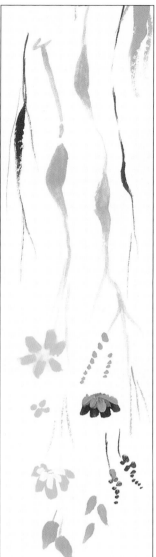

Dried stems: Use the no. 0 liner to paint stems and small leaves (as shown above) with Lichen Grey, Dark Foliage Green, Charcoal and Deep Lilac + Charcoal.

Flowers: Paint petals with comma strokes using the no. 3 round brush. Place darker petals on the bottom of each flower and lighter petals on the top using Straw and Old Parchment, Deep Lilac and Lavender Lace, and Cape Cod Blue and Lavender Lace.

Twine: Use the no. 0 liner with Burnt Umber, Lichen Grey and White, thinned to an inky consistency.

Varnish with Delta Exterior/Interior Varnish according to the manufacturer's instructions.

Dusty
Mauve

Deep Lilac

Charcoal

Cayenne

Cape Cod
Blue

Burnt
Umber

Bridgeport
Grey

Black Green

Light Ivory

Light Foliage
Green

Medium
Foliage Green

Dark Foliage
Green

COTTAGE
GARDEN SHOP

*The charming,
thatch-roofed cottage
on this shovel is
similar to one
I spotted in Carmel,
California.
Surrounded by
greenery and flowers,
the "Cottage Garden
Shop," makes
for a scene right
out of a storybook.*

Supplies:
Decorative rusty shovel
Delta Metal Primer
Delta Exterior/Interior
  Varnish
Brushes:
no. 10/0 liner
no. 3 round
no. 4 short flat
no. 2 filbert

nos. 2, 8, 10 flats
Old no. 8 short flat
1-inch (25mm) wash
  brush

Prep: Sand handle, then
using the wash brush,
paint it using Stonewedge
Green + a touch of
Bridgeport Grey.

Metal: Sand, wipe
clean, wash with
soap and water, then
rinse with vinegar.
Let dry. Apply Delta
Metal Primer with a
1-inch (25mm) wash
brush, following
instructions on the
label. Sand lightly.

Apply pattern of
house, roof,
windows and fence
with white graphite
paper and a stylus.

Lichen Grey

Lavender Lace

Old Parchment

Payne's Grey

Rosetta Pink

Stonewedge Green

Wedgwood Green

Straw

White

Woodland Night Green

Dark Burnt Umber

Nightfall Blue

House: Basecoat using a no. 2 and no. 8 flat brush. Two coats may be necessary for good coverage. For dark areas use Cape Cod Blue; medium areas (fence), Cape Cod Blue + Lavender Lace 2:1; light areas, Cape Cod Blue + Lavender Lace + White 2:1:1.

Roof: Use a no. 8 flat brush with a "dirty brush mixing" technique: Don't clean the brush between color changes. Work wet-on-wet, blending one value into the other. For dark areas use Charcoal; medium areas, Charcoal + Lichen Grey; light areas, Lichen Grey.

Thatch: Side load no. 8 flat brush with Dark Burnt Umber. Turn the project sideways. Using the chisel stroke (see page 7) start at the top far right end of the roof. Continue down the length of the roof. For lighter thatch, use Lichen Grey + a touch of Burnt Umber. With Lichen Grey + a touch of Burnt Umber, softly glaze (see page 6) the top and center of the roof, the entrance overhang, and above the window on the left.

Windows: Paint inside the windows with a no. 8 flat brush and Charcoal. Paint shutters on the right front and sides of the house with a no. 2 flat brush and White. Paint shutters on the left side of the house and shade under both eaves using Bridgeport Grey + White.

Trace on the rest of pattern omitting sign.

Flower boxes: Use a no. 2 flat brush to paint the fronts White + Bridgeport Grey, the right sides White, and the inside Bridgeport Grey.

Curtains: Use a no. 8 flat brush with Lichen Grey to paint softly. Let some of the Charcoal show through.

Windows, frames and panes: Use a no. 10/0 brush with White for the wider frame and Bridgeport Grey for individual frames. Thin paint to an inky consistency for fine lines. Turn the project sideways to make it easier to do horizontal lines.

Entranceway: Double load a no. 8 flat brush with Payne's Grey and Cape Cod Blue. Apply Payne's Grey down the left side at an angle (see above).

Trees: Use an old no. 8 short flat brush side-loaded with Black Green and Woodland Night Green and for variety use Dark Foliage Green and Wedgwood Green. With the lighter value at the top and the darker value at the bottom, start in the sky and work down to the roof, patting in half circles, from 9 o'clock to 3 o'clock and back (see "foliage" stroke on page 8).

Stairs: Paint the top of the stairs with a no. 4 short flat and Lichen Grey and under the stairs with Lichen Grey + Charcoal.

Pathway: (optional) Paint with Lichen Grey, Charcoal and Burnt Umber with a no. 8 flat. Slide the brush back and forth forming an irregular curvy path, blending the colors together.

Fence and flower buckets: With a no. 2 flat, base the buckets with Cape Cod Blue + Lavender Lace. With a no. 10/0 liner, paint lines on buckets of Cape Cod Blue + Lavender Lace + White 1:1:1. Shade under buckets with a side load float (see page 7) of Nightfall Blue. Stipple in greenery of Medium Foliage Green and flowers of Dusty Mauve and Rosetta Pink.

Shrubbery and vines: Use a double-loaded old worn no. 8 short flat to stipple vines and foliage (see "foliage" stroke page 8). Use Light Foliage Green and Dark Foliage Green. As you work forward, use Medium Foliage Green and Light Foliage Green + a touch of Light Ivory.

Pots at end of pathway: Base with Cayenne + Rosetta Pink using a no. 8 flat brush. Paint light areas Rosetta Pink + White, blending into, but not covering, the previous color. Shade the sides with Burnt Umber. Shade under the pots with Dark Burnt Umber. Stipple greenery in pots with Dark Foliage Green and Light Foliage Green. Paint the pot in the doorway with Cayenne. Stipple in Medium Foliage Green for greenery.

Flowers: Paint small comma strokes for the flowers using a no. 2 filbert. For the violet flowers, use Deep Lilac and White. For the white flowers, use Light Ivory and White. For the yellow flowers, use Straw and Old Parchment and for the pink flowers, use Dusty Mauve and White.

For the hollyhocks use Deep Lilac, Dusty Mauve and Rosetta Pink dots.

Doorway vines and flowers: Using a no. 3 round and Deep Lilac, stipple flowers. Highlight with Deep Lilac + White. Stipple in greenery with a no. 3 round and Woodland Night and Wedgwood Green.

Sign: Trace on pattern. With a no. 3 round, base the posts with Lichen Grey. Shade with Burnt Umber. Base the sign with Lichen Grey. Letter with a no. 10/0 liner and Dark Burnt Umber, thinned to an inky consistency.

Apply several coats of Delta Exterior/Interior Varnish according to the manufacturer's instructions.

The Cottage Garden Shop

Shovel Pattern

Pitchfork Pattern

19

Straw

Lichen Grey

Burnt Umber

Dark Burnt Umber

Tomato Spice

Vintage Wine

Dark Foliage Green

Stonewedge Green

Light Foliage Green

DREAM GARDEN

If only my own home garden was as enchanting as this one! This metal bucket has provided a place for a painted dream garden, complete with a charming scarecrow and pre-picked basket full of bounty. Vegetables and flowers are included in this design, along with a variety of birds.

If you love a lot of fine detail, you'll enjoy working on this project, and this bucket will be a scene-stealer wherever you place it. It makes a wonderful planter, of course, but you can also use it for creative food presentation, as a napkin holder, or…it's up to you!

Supplies:

Metal bucket
Delta Metal Primer
Delta Exterior/Interior Varnish
Brushes:
no. 10/0 liner
no. 3 round
no. 2 filbert
nos. 2, 8 flats
1-inch (25mm) wash
Old worn no. 8 short flat

Salem Blue

Deep Lilac

Charcoal

Heritage
Green

GP Purple

Lilac

Bungalow
Blue

Mello Yellow

Woodland
Night Green

Blue Haze

Peachy Keen

Cactus
Green

Magnolia
White

Prep: Follow previous metal instruction. With a 1-inch (25mm) wash brush, base the bucket with Stonewedge Green, inside and out.

Sky and greenery: Use a no. 8 flat and Salem Blue to base sky. Blend in Blue Haze to horizon line. Base tree line with Woodland Night Green and then Salem Green to below fence.

Garden area: With a no. 8 flat, slip-slap with Burnt Umber. Work down to middle areas and add Burnt Umber + Lichen Grey. In light areas in foreground, add Burnt Umber + Peachy Keen.

Apply fence pattern.

Background trees: Double load the old worn no. 8 short flat with Cactus Green on the top and Woodland Night Green on the bottom. Stipple rows of trees unevenly using a "foliage" stroke (see page 8). Continue with both colors to the far right of the fence and down to the garden area. On the outside left of the fence, stipple in the trees with Light and Dark Foliage Green. Paint the grass area below the trees with Cactus Green + Salem Blue using a no. 8 flat brush.

Fence: With a no. 3 round, base the logs with Burnt Umber. Highlight with the chisel edge of the no. 8 flat and Lichen Grey. Shade the logs with Dark Burnt Umber.

Apply pattern for garden.

Flowers: Double load a no. 8 flat with Light Foliage Green and Dark Foliage Green. Stipple in the leafy area, keeping light on top. With a no. 3 round, tap in flowers of Lilac + Magnolia White, Lilac, Deep Lilac, Bungalow Blue, Vintage Wine and Mello Yellow. Tap in the darker colors, then highlight with the lighter colors. Use the no. 10/0 for stems and fine leaves.

Apply detailed pattern.

Lettuce: Double load a no. 8 flat with Light Foliage Green on the top and Dark Foliage Green on the bottom to make comma strokes (see page 7), first from left to the center, then right to left (see above right).

Leafy greens: Double load the brush as above, and make zigzag strokes (see above and page 8).

Corn: Base stalks with thick and thin strokes of Light and Dark Foliage Green. Base corn with Straw and highlight with Mello Yellow.

Lavender: With a no. 10/0 liner, stroke in leaves and stems using Dark and Light Foliage Green. Add dots of Deep Lilac, highlighted with Lilac + Magnolia White.

Other foliage: Use a no. 3 round and stipple and pounce. Use a no. 10/0 liner for long leaves and stems. Add your own flowers and vegetables.

Scarecrow: With a no. 2 flat and Burnt Umber, paint in wooden pole. Base the hat with Straw, and highlight with Mello Yellow. Paint the shirt Tomato Spice with stripes of Magnolia White. Paint the straw stuffing with a no. 10/0 liner and Straw, and highlight with Mello Yellow. Base the pants with Bungalow Blue + Magnolia White. Outline and shade with Bungalow Blue.

Rooster: Base with a no. 2 filbert and GP Purple. To paint feathers, start at tail and work toward the front. Don't wash brush between colors, just let values blend.

 With the no. 2 filbert, paint large commas of Vintage Wine at tail, then smaller ones working up under the chest and neck. Overlay with Deep Lilac comma strokes. Paint the wing and back area with comma strokes of Lilac highlighted with Lilac + Magnolia White. Paint Bungalow Blue comma strokes in middle area. Paint the beak Straw and the comb Tomato Spice with a no. 10/0.

Chicks: Base in Straw with a no. 2 filbert. Highlight with Mello Yellow.

Blue chicken and blue bird: Base with a no. 3 round and Bungalow Blue. Highlight with Bungalow Blue + Magnolia White. Paint the beak Straw and the comb Tomato Spice using a no. 10/0.

Basket of flowers and corn: Base with a no. 2 flat and Raw Sienna. For weave, tap in Peachy Keen. Shade under curve of handle with Burnt Umber. Softly float under basket with Dark Burnt Umber. Add flowers and corn using the same colors used throughout the design.

Wired fence: With the no. 10/0 liner, paint the wire Bungalow Blue with highlights of Lichen Grey.

Shovel: Using the chisel edge of a no. 8 flat, base the handle with Burnt Umber + Peachy Keen. Highlight with Peachy Keen. Shade with Dark Burnt Umber. Base the metal with Charcoal + Magnolia White. Shade with Charcoal and highlight with Magnolia White.

Dirt under shovel: Paint Burnt Umber and highlight with Peachy Keen.

Spray with Delta Exterior/Interior Varnish.

Enlarge Pattern 150%

WISTFUL VISTA

This tall, rusted-metal bucket offers a large space on which to paint a richly detailed, vertical scene. I've really indulged my love of wisteria here, winding the vines up and across a wooden trellis. The scene includes a rustic bridge crossing a brook, some gardening tools and lots of planted flowers. This restful place certainly beckons to me. I picture myself sitting on a porch enjoying this view for hours!

I would display this piece holding an ample bouquet of fresh or dried flowers. It could also be used as an umbrella stand or other storage bin.

Supplies:

Rusted metal bucket
Delta Metal Primer
Delta Faux Finish Glaze Base

Delta Exterior/Interior
    Varnish, spray or brush-on
2¹/₂" (6.35 cm) sponge

Brushes:
no. 10/0 liner
no. 3 round
no. 8 short round
nos. 2, 8 filberts
nos. 2, 8 flats
no. 4 short flat
1-inch (25mm) mop
1-inch (25mm) wash

Dark Forest Green

Deep Lilac

Dusty Purple

Magnolia White

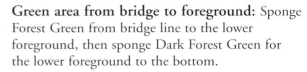

Forest Green

Hammered Iron

Dark Burnt Umber

Chocolate Cherry

Cape Cod Blue

Burnt Umber

Bridgeport Grey

Blue Heaven

Lilac

Prep: Follow the instructions on the label for the Metal Primer medium. Wash, then rinse with vinegar. Sand lightly to smooth surface. Wipe off residue using a dampened cloth. Mark on the surface where the horizon is to be, using white graphite paper and a stylus.

Sky: Use a 1-inch (25mm) wash brush and large mop brush for blending the colors together. With the wash brush and Cape Cod Blue, slip-slap the upper part of the sky and down both sides of the trellis areas. Use Blue Heaven to slip-slap from the Cape Cod Blue to the horizon line. Use the mop brush to pounce up and down to blend the two values together.

Background trees: Dampen a sponge, then dry it on a towel. Sponge softly and lightly using Lilac for distant tree line. Middle row of trees: Forest Green. Lower row: Dark Forest Green.

Green area from bridge to foreground: Sponge Forest Green from bridge line to the lower foreground, then sponge Dark Forest Green for the lower foreground to the bottom.

Apply the pattern using white graphite paper and a stylus.

Trellis: Use a no. 8 flat brush and base with Burnt Umber (imperfect lines will be covered up with the wisteria.) Lighten top or outer edges with Lichen Grey using the chisel edge of brush.

Wisteria: Tap left sides of cluster with the no. 8 short brush and Dusty Purple. Wipe excess off the brush. Tap right sides with Deep Lilac for medium values. Wipe brush. Tap Lilac gently for light values, forming clusters. Let previous values show through. Highlight some clusters with Pink Quartz. Tap in greenery with Heritage Green. Paint tendrils with a no. 10/0 liner and Lichen Grey.

Hat: Load the no. 8 flat brush with Straw and base the hat. Shade with Raw Sienna on the left sides and top indentation. Highlight with Mello Yellow on the top area. Use the no. 2 flat for band and ribbon. Base with Magenta; highlight with Magenta + Magnolia White at the curve and outer right edges.

24

Heritage Green

Lichen Grey

Magenta

Mello Yellow

Pink Quartz

Raw Sienna

Raw Linen

Royal Fuchsia

Purple Smoke

Straw

Wedgwood Green

Woodland Night Green

Bungalow Blue

Sidalcea (pink flowers): Start with the flowers in the background. Double load a no. 8 flat brush with Royal Fuchsia and Magnolia White. Zigzag three to four strokes (see page 8), pick up brush. Paint another three to four strokes until you complete the circle or half circle. For the centers, use a no. 10/0 liner with Chocolate Cherry to create a five star effect. For buds and stems, use Chocolate Cherry + Burnt Umber. Highlight buds with Royal Fuchsia. Make a variety of sizes, overlapping some.

Tree fern: Double load a no. 8 flat brush. Paint the forward fronds with Dark Forest Green and Wedgwood. For the fronds on left side use Woodland Night Green and Heritage Green. Use the chisel edge of the brush to paint the ferns (see page 7).

Bridge and fence: Use a no. 4 short bright brush to base the back posts using Burnt Umber + a touch of Cape Cod Blue. For the front posts and fence use Burnt Umber. Highlight the bridge's front posts with Lichen Grey.

Haze over the bridge: Apply Glaze Medium to the surface, then glaze in Mello Yellow for haze over top of the bridge in the tree line.

Rocky riverbed: Use a no. 8 filbert to casually lay in the rocks. Paint the background rocks grayer and smaller. Paint them bigger and more colorful in the foreground. Use Burnt Umber, Hammered Iron and Lichen Grey. Let dry. Apply glaze medium over rocks. Paint a shear glaze of Blue Heaven "water" over and around the rocks.

Garden rows: Double load a no. 4 short flat brush with Forest Green and Dark Forest Green for the background, and Wedgwood Green and Forest Green for the foreground. Use Lichen Grey streaks for dirt paths. Tap in colors of your choice for the flowers. It's your garden.

Green field and flowers: Use green previously used and create a variety of colors for flowers.

Viola Pedata (blue flowers): Use a no. 8 filbert and base with Bungalow Blue. Shade with Purple Smoke. Use Bungalow Blue + Magnolia White to lighten top petals where they overlap. For front face petal, use liner and Magnolia White to paint fine lines shaped into a "V." For stamen, use the liner brush and Magnolia White. Highlight center with dots of Mello Yellow.

Gloriosa daisy: Load a no. 3 round or no. 2 filbert with Straw. Then gently tip into Magnolia White. Start at the top petals and paint a set of three petals. Reload to continue each set.

Hollyhocks: Use a no. 3 round with Dark Forest Green for stems. For leaves, double load a no. 8 flat brush with Wedgwood Green and Dark Forest Green and use a zigzag stroke (see page 8). Suggested flower colors: Royal Fuchsia, Dusty Purple, Bungalow Blue; center, Chocolate Cherry + Burnt Umber. Highlight with Pink Quartz, then Magnolia White + color used.

Black-eyed Susans: Use a no. 3 round with Wedgwood Green and Medium Foliage Green to paint the stems. For the petals use Mello Yellow + Straw. Start at the center of the flower and pull out to curvy, thin points. For centers, base with Dark Burnt Umber in high circles. Stipple on the top left with Raw Sienna.

White flowers: Use a no. 3 round and Raw Linen to base flowers. Shade with Bridgeport Grey. Use Straw for the center, shaded with Dark Forest Green.

Shovel and rake: Use a no. 4 short flat to base handles using Burnt Umber + Magnolia White. Shade with Burnt Umber and Dark Burnt Umber, outlining the edges. Base the shovel's rusted metal with Burnt Umber + Magnolia White. For the rake's metal, base with Bridgeport Grey + Magnolia White. Shade and outline under rake handle with Charcoal. Shade on ground, under the shovel and rake using Dark Burnt Umber.

Varnish with Delta Exterior/Interior Varnish.

Alpine Green

 Bahama Purple

 Black Green

 Burnt Umber

 Chocolate Cherry

 Dark Foliage Green

HERBS DE PROVENCE

Planted with a variety of herbs, this makes a wonderful gift, if you can bear to part with it! Imagine this box in a sunny kitchen window or atop a table in a gazebo or patio.

I've provided instructions for painting mint, thyme, rosemary, sage, lavender, and curry, but you can always improvise your own designs to include your favorites.

Supplies:

Rusted planter
Delta Metal Primer
Delta Exterior/Interior
  Varnish

Brushes:
no. 10/0 liner
no. 3 round
no. 8 short round

no. 8 flat
no. 4 short flat
1-inch (25mm) wash

28

Eggshell White

Hydrangea Pink

Lichen Grey

Light Foliage Green

Lilac

Magenta

Medium Foliage Green

Mello Yellow

Raw Linen

Raw Sienna

Wisteria

Prep: Follow the instructions on the label for the Metal Primer medium. Wash, then rinse with vinegar. Sand lightly. Wipe off residue using a dampened cloth. With white graphite paper and a stylus, apply only the letter part of the pattern.

Letters: Base with Lichen Grey. Shade around the edges with Burnt Umber to give the letters depth.

Paint the names of the herbs at the bottom of the planter with a no. 10/0 liner and Alpine Green.

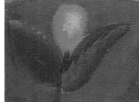

Apply rest of pattern.

Mint

Stems: Base stems with a no. 3 round with Burnt Umber + Chocolate Cherry, thinned to an inky consistency.

Folded-over leaves: Paint backside of leaf first with Dark Foliage Green on the no 8 flat. Wiggle the brush and pull up onto the tip of the brush to create "pointed" leaf ends. For the front of folded leaf, double load a no. 8 flat. Place Light Foliage Green at the top and Medium Foliage Green at the bottom.

Flat leaves: Double load the no. 8 flat with Light Foliage Green on top and Medium Foliage Green on the bottom. Flip the brush over so the dark value is again in the center and repeat the stroke.

Flowers: With a no. 8 short round, stipple the flowers with Wisteria. Stipple Lilac into the centers, blending the values together.

Center highlight: Stipple Lilac + a touch of Raw Linen, offset slightly to the right of the center. Tap to blend the values together. Wipe off excess paint on towel then continue blending.

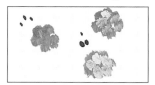

Thyme

Stems: Base stems using a no. 3 round with Burnt Umber + Chocolate Cherry.

Leaves: With a no. 4 short flat, double load Light and Dark Foliage Green. Hold the brush vertically to paint the leaves. The larger leaves point downward. The small little leaves at the base of the flower are little S-strokes pointing down.

Flowers: With a no. 3 round, stipple in Magenta, then stipple in highlights with Hydrangea Pink. With the tip of the brush, make two to three little pollen dots with Chocolate Cherry + Burnt Umber at the ends of the flowers.

Sage

Stems: With a no. 3 round, base stems Alpine Green + a touch of Medium Foliage Green. Shade at the sides and bottom with Burnt Umber.

Leaves: With a no. 8 flat, repeat the leaf strokes as for the mint. Lay one leaf over another to create depth.

Paint the background leaves Dark Foliage Green + a touch of Alpine Green. Paint the middle leaves with Medium Foliage Green and the front leaves Medium Foliage Green + Light Foliage Green.

Flowers: Using a no. 3 round, paint the back petals with Lichen Grey comma strokes. Tap the light areas with Lichen Grey + Raw Linen. Create a variety of petals. Tap in highlights with Raw Linen.

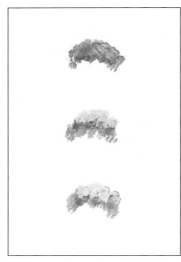

Rosemary

Stems: Base stems with a no. 3 round using Burnt Umber.

Leaves: Use a no. 10/0 liner and start with the Dark Foliage Green. Paint more leaves with Medium Foliage Green, then Light Foliage Green. Thin the paint to an inky consistency. Turn project upside down and pull the strokes up, out and toward you. Cross lines over one another for depth.

Flowers: With a no. 3 round and Bahama Purple, paint small comma strokes. Highlight with Eggshell White.

Curry

Stems: With a no. 10/0 liner, paint stems Alpine Green. For darker stems, use Black Green and softly glaze with Alpine Green to darken some areas. With the liner, paint leaves using Alpine Green (see picture above).

Flowers: Stipple flowers using a no. 3 round with Raw Sienna. Lighten with Mello Yellow. Highlight with Eggshell White on tip.

Varnish with Delta Exterior/Interior Varnish.

Lavender

Stems: With a no. 10/0 liner and thinned Black Green + a touch of Alpine Green, paint long stems, pulling up from bottom. Paint curved leaves, always starting from the center of the stem.

Flowers: Using the no. 3 round, stipple the back petals first with Chocolate Cherry. Then stipple with Wisteria, and highlight with Lilac.

Mint   Thyme

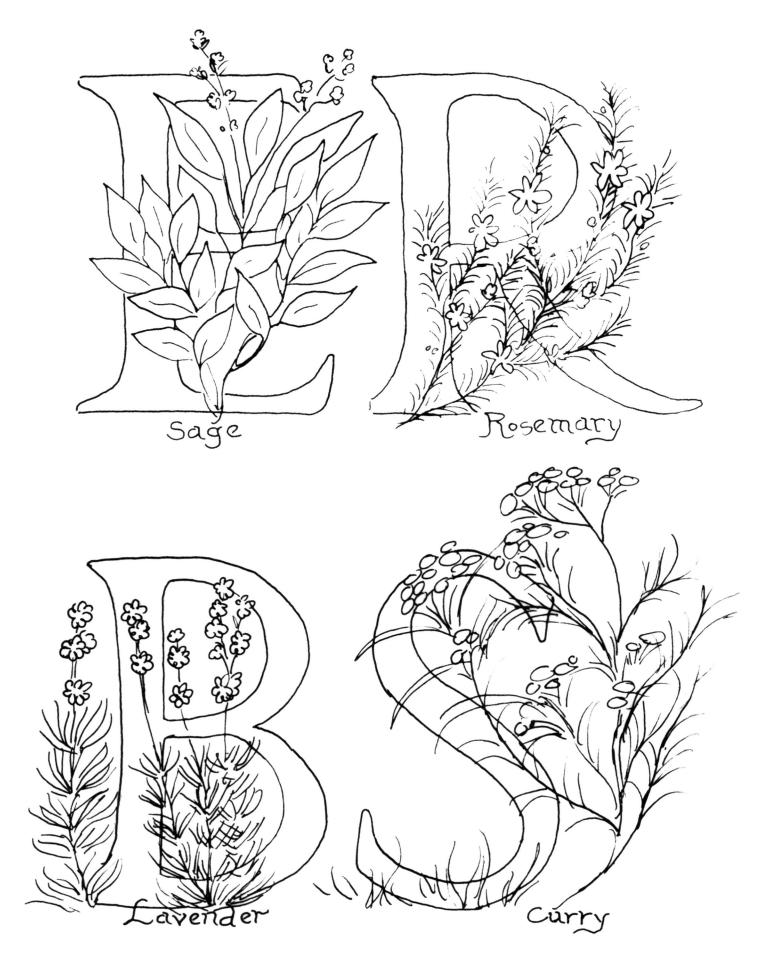

Sage

Rosemary

Lavender

Curry

PAT'S WATERING CAN

I love the mix of Stonewedge Green with the natural rust on this watering can, so I strove for a balance of painted and unpainted areas. The soft purples and blues work wonderfully with this pretty green.

This project is an example of a useful tool that can become a very charming, decorative accessory in your sunroom or patio. In the painted scene, a variety of delicate flowers grow from a lush, grassy base, and a dried bouquet hangs overhead. These dainty blooms are easy to create with just a few strokes!

Felicia
Spring Merchant...

© Patricia Eisenbraun 2...

PAT'S WATERING CAN

Burnt Umber

Cape Cod Blue

Supplies:

Galvanized/rusty watering can
Delta Metal Primer
Delta Exterior/Interior Varnish

Brushes:
no. 10/0 liner
no. 3 round
nos. 2, 8 flats
1-inch (25 mm) wash brush
Old no. 8 short flat

Prep: Follow the instructions on the label for the Metal Primer. Wash with soap and water. Rinse in vinegar. Let dry. Apply Metal Primer with 1-inch (25mm) wash brush. Let dry. Sand lightly to smooth surface and wipe with a damp cloth.

Basecoat: Using the 1-inch (25mm) wash brush and Stonewedge Green + Raw Linen 2:1, apply several thin coats.

Apply pattern: Apply pattern with the white graphite paper and a stylus. Look under pattern to check for heavy lines. Don't apply too much pressure.

| Dark Foliage Green | Deep Lilac | Eggplant | Forest Green | Lichen Grey | Old Parchment |

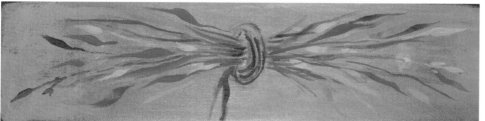  

Raw Linen

Dried bouquets: For stems, use a no. 10/0 liner brush and Stonewedge Green and Burnt Umber to create thin-thick lines and long-short stems. Overlap and swing out to sides.

For twine, use a no. 3 round brush and Burnt Umber to create easy half circle lines. Highlight with Lichen Grey. Pull and twist brush to create ends of twine.

Stonewedge Green

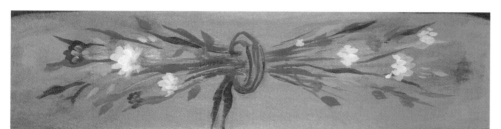 

Straw

Flowers in bouquet: Use the no. 3 round brush to paint comma strokes for flowers. Paint the darker value first, then place the lighter value on top.

Yellow flowers: Old Parchment on the bottom and Straw + White on top.
Purple flowers: Eggplant on the bottom and Raw Linen on top.
Blue flowers: Cape Cod Blue on the bottom and Raw Linen on top.

White

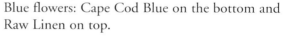

Light Foliage Green

Seed packets: Use a no. 8 flat brush to basecoat the top half using Lichen Grey. Use Cape Cod Blue + Raw Linen for the sides and bottom. Use Payne's Grey for the center, shading at the bottom and edges. Outline the top of the packages with Burnt Umber.

Lettering: Use a no. 10/0 liner and Burnt Umber thinned with water to an inky consistency.

Hyssop: Use a no. 10/0 liner brush and Forest Green + Light Foliage for stems. Use a no. 3 round brush and Eggplant to stipple flowers. Stipple again with Deep Lilac + White, but don't cover the previous color. On Dill package, paint little squares of Forest Green + Light Foliage Green with a no. 2 flat brush. On Hyssop package, dot around edge with Deep Lilac. (See photo of finished project, page 34.)

Payne's Grey

Dill bouquet: Use a no. 10/0 liner brush and Forest Green + a touch of Light Foliage Green for the stems. Pull from the center of the stem, then curve up and out.

At the top of the stems, tap in curved little florets using a no. 3 round brush and Forest Green.

Tap Light Foliage Green on top, keeping the florets airy and light. Highlight with Old Parchment.

Felicia daisies: Use a no. 3 round brush and Forest Green + a touch of Light Foliage Green to create thin-thick stems. Paint comma strokes with Raw Linen for the flowers. Dot the centers with Straw, highlight with White and shade with Burnt Umber. For the small flowers on the package, use Raw Linen and Old Parchment.

Paint comma strokes of Deep Lilac + White for the violet flowers. Use Cape Cod Blue + a touch of Raw Linen for the blue flowers. Glaze over the petals of the white daisies with Deep Lilac + White.

Bottom foliage: Use an old worn no. 8 short flat brush to stipple in the space at the bottom with Burnt Umber. Stipple the foliage with the brush double-loaded with Light Foliage Green and Dark Foliage Green. Pounce in uneven half circles, keeping the Light Foliage Green on top (see "foliage" stroke, page 8).

Varnish with Delta Exterior/Interior Varnish according to the manufacturer's instructions.

WELCOME HOME

Every inch of this wooden birdhouse has been painted, starting with a white basecoat stained with blue and peach and finishing with many garden-themed renderings. Note the crackled roof and the faux rocks on the bottom and around the openings. Texture Builder was used to create "mortar," which you can actually feel with your fingertips.

Details include topiary trees, gardening tools, a window and lots of flowers, including my favorite, wisteria.

This decorative piece can also be functional. An opening in the back allows you to insert a bulb inside and use it as a night-light.

Dark Foliage
Green

Dusty
Mauve

Nightfall
Blue

Hippo Grey

Medium
Foliage Green

Light Foliage
Green

Charcoal

Cayenne

Cape Cod
Blue

Burnt
Umber

Pink Quartz

Antique
Gold

White

WELCOME HOME

Prep: Sand the surface. Wipe off residue with a dampened cloth. Seal using a 1-inch (25mm) wash brush and sealer.

Roof: With Cape Cod Blue and a 1-inch (25mm) wash brush, paint the roof top, sides and under the eaves. Paint the three dowels with Cape Cod Blue.

Walls: Paint all four sides White.

Base of birdhouse: Paint Hippo Grey.

Sheer streaks on walls: Using a no. 8 flat brush, apply sheer streaks down the walls first with Cape Cod Blue then with Rosetta Pink. Thin the paint on the palette paper to a very watery consistency before applying.

Crackled roof: Using a 1-inch (25mm) wash brush, apply the Crackle Medium according to directions on package. Pull the brush in one direction. Try not to go over previously applied areas. Let dry, then apply one sheer coat of White. Make it streaky, allowing the blue to show through.

Supplies:
Wooden birdhouse
Delta All Purpose Sealer
Delta Satin Exterior/Interior
  Varnish
Delta Crackle Medium
Delta Texture Builder
Cotton swabs

Brushes:
no. 10/0 liner
no. 3 round
no. 8 short round
nos. 2, 8 filberts
nos. 2, 8 flats
1-inch (25mm) wash
  brush
Old worn no. 8 flat

Lichen Grey

Lavender

Old Parchment

Peachy Keen

Bridgeport Grey

Wisteria

Raw Sienna

Rosetta Pink

Salem Blue

Sandstone

Stonewedge Green

Straw

Vintage Wine

Rocks: With the no. 8 filbert, paint rocks Hippo Grey, Burnt Umber, Sandstone, Raw Sienna and Cayenne. Don't worry about the shape of the rocks, just dab on the colors.

Mortar: Mix Delta's Texture Builder + Hippo Grey 1:1 with a palette knife. With an old brush, scoop up this "mortar" and apply in irregular shapes around the rocks. At this time, apply the rocks and mortar around the opening for the night-light at the back of the house.

Pots: With a no. 8 short round, base entire area with Cayenne. Stipple an area of Peachy Keen for a highlight in the center. Stipple to shade the sides and bottoms of the pots with Burnt Umber. Blend the edges of the values for a soft transition.

Topiary: With a no. 8 short, stipple the entire circle with Medium Foliage Green.

Tap a highlight of Light Foliage off-center. Wipe excess paint from the brush onto a towel. Softly blend edges of values together with the brush. Shade by stippling Dark Foliage Green on the sides of the topiary that are away from the door.

Use the chisel edge of the no. 8 flat to paint the trunks with Burnt Umber (first picture). Lighten the centers with Lichen Grey (second picture), blending the two colors together (third picture).

Flowers in topiary pots: With a no. 3 round, dab in some greenery of Dark Foliage Green and Stonewedge Green. Create a bouquet of flowers with comma strokes using Wisteria, Vintage Wine, Dusty Mauve and Old Parchment. Add White to any color to lighten.

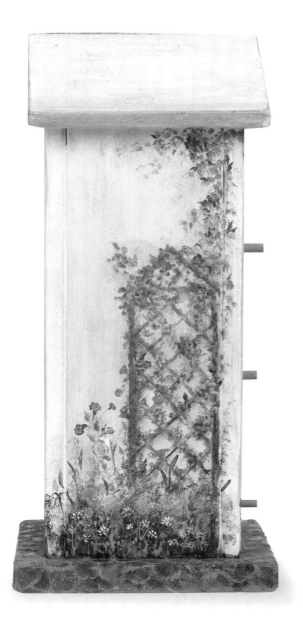

Trellis: With the no. 3 round, base in the trellis with White + Charcoal. Note that the outer boards are thicker than the crisscross slats.

Wisteria: Paint the wisteria on all sides of the house, then paint the wisteria on the trellis. Use either a no. 8 short round brush or cotton swabs to create the flowers. If using a short round, tap straight into the color, and dab excess on a towel. Tap on the project forming soft, delicate clumps. If using cotton swabs, get the cotton wet, pinch out the moisture, and mold in your fingers to tighten the cotton. Tap straight into the paint. Tap on palette paper until you get the look you want. Tap on the project to form delicate clusters. Tapping harder forms more rounded, and sometimes transparent, clusters. You can double load the cotton swabs like a brush. Use Vintage Wine and Lavender, then add a few accent clusters of Dusty Mauve and White to lighten. Lightly stipple the leaves with the no. 8 short round or cotton swabs. With a no. 3 round, paint small leaf strokes of Light Foliage Green, Medium Foliage Green and some Salem Blue for cool accents. Use the no. 10/0 liner for tendrils.

Sponged grass: Tape over the rock area to protect it.

Dampen the sponge and dry well on a towel. Dab the sponge into the paint and dab the excess on a paper towel. Tap the sponge on your palette until the desired look is achieved. The grass is the basis for the flowers to grow out of.

Begin by tapping Salem Blue very lightly in the background. Next, lightly tap in Light Foliage Green. Working down, tap in Medium Foliage Green, and finish with Medium Foliage Green + Nightfall Blue at the bottom.

Flowers in the grass: Use a no. 3 round to create your own garden: Paint morning glories of Cape Cod Blue and outline with Nightfall Blue; daisies of Old Parchment and Straw; add other flowers with Rosetta Pink, Wisteria and Vintage Wine and White to lighten.

Leaves and stems: With a no. 10/0 liner, create stems and leaves with Light Foliage Green and Medium Foliage Green.

Straw hat: With a no. 8 flat, base the hat with Straw. Shade with a side-loaded float of Raw Sienna. Highlight the left side with Straw + White, then just White. Shade on the wall with a side-loaded float of Charcoal. With a no. 2 flat, paint the band with Dusty Mauve. Start on the chisel, slide the brush down, apply pressure at the curve, and slide the chisel up to make a circle. Use the same color and brush to paint long S-strokes for the ribbons.

Herb boards: With the no. 8 flat, base with Raw Sienna. With a no. 10/0 liner, outline the dowels with Burnt Umber. With the no. 8 flat, chisel in grain lines with Burnt Umber. Shade around dowels with a side-loaded float of Burnt Umber. Highlight the centers of the dowels with Straw. Shade under the board with a side-loaded float of Charcoal.

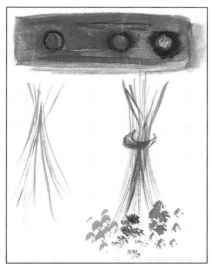

Dried stems and flowers: With a no. 10/0 liner, pull thin stems with Medium Foliage Green + Stonewedge Green. Add some with Burnt Umber. With a no. 3 round, stipple flowers with Vintage Wine, Dusty Mauve, Stonewedge Green and White to lighten. Swirl in strings around the bundles using a no. 10/0 liner and thinned Raw Sienna and Burnt Umber.

Gloves: Use a no. 3 round for all the following steps. Base in the dowel with Raw Sienna. Base the gloves with Straw. Shade Raw Sienna between the fingers, folds and around the dowel. Highlight the top folds with Straw + White. Add decorative dots of Stonewedge Green. Highlight with Straw.

Shovel, rake and watering can: Base the handles with the no. 3 round and Burnt Umber. Highlight the middle of the handles with Raw Sienna. For metal, base with Bridgeport Grey using a no. 8 or no. 2 flat. Lighten areas with Bridgeport Grey + White; shade with Bridgeport Grey + Charcoal.

Flowers at base of house: With a no. 10/0 liner and no. 3 round, create a variety of flowers with Vintage Wine and Wisteria; use Pink Quartz for highlights. Add Dusty Mauve for a few scattered accents. With a no. 10/0 liner, paint Stonewedge Green leaves and foliage. Wipe excess paint off brush onto towel frequently.

Window frames and flower box: With a no. 8 flat, base the outer frames and box with Cape Cod Blue + Sandstone 2:1. Let dry. Shade with a side-loaded float of Nightfall Blue around the frame edges. Glaze in soft floats of Charcoal inside the window for background depth. With an almost dry brush loaded with Peachy Keen, brush over the "glass" at an angle.

Curtains: Side load the no. 8 flat with White. Turn project sideways. Place the paint side of the brush toward the flower box and slide the brush making irregular half circles. Slide up the chisel to create folds. With an almost dry brush loaded with White, brush a reflection over the windows and curtains at an angle.

Window sashes: Base the sashes and the center frame with Cape Cod Blue + a touch of Sandstone. For the center frame use a no. 2 flat. For the sashes, use a no. 10/0 liner.

Flower box greens: With a no. 3 round, stipple in leaves with Light Foliage Green and Medium Foliage Green + a touch of Stonewedge Green.

Flowers in flower box: With a no. 3 round, tap in delicate flowers with Vintage Wine and Wisteria. Add daisies of Old Parchment with centers of Dusty Mauve. Create your own bouquet.

Let dry for 24 hours. Apply several coats of spray varnish or brush-on varnish. Dry between each coat.

Hint:
Follow the instructions in this book, but feel free to add your own touches or to change colors if you wish. Remember that your own painted piece will be a one-of-a-kind original. Be sure to sign and date your piece when it's completed.

Top

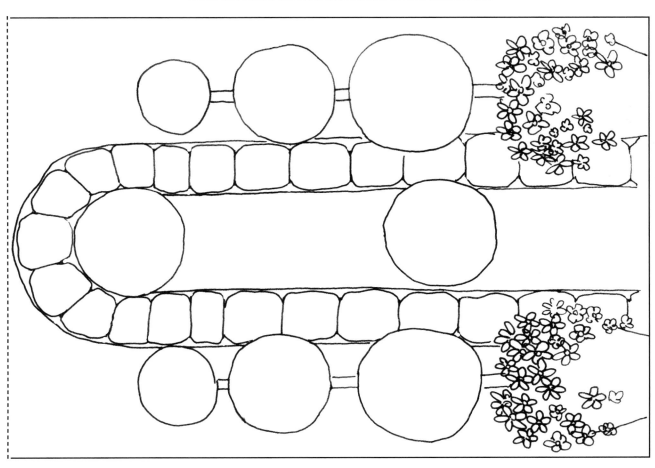

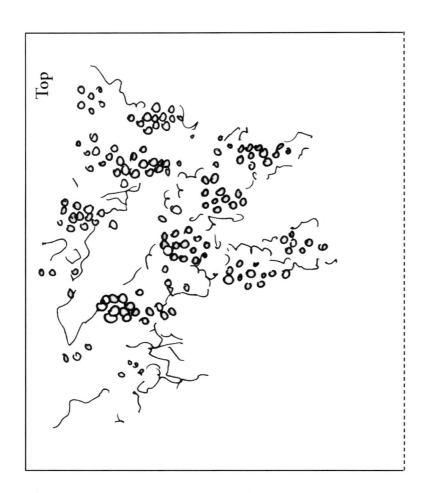

Top

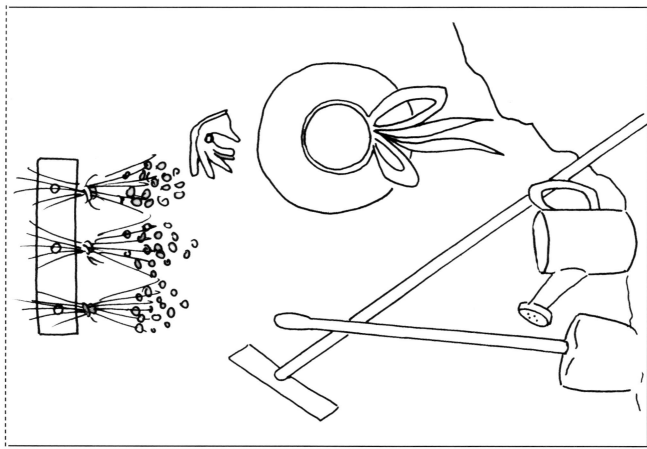

Pattern for side of Birdhouse

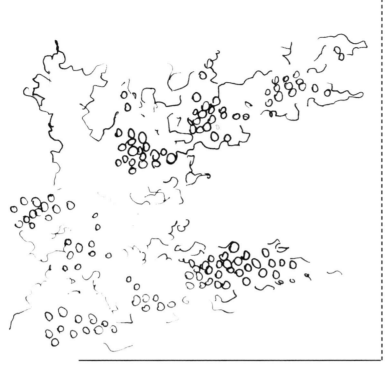

Pattern for back of Birdhouse

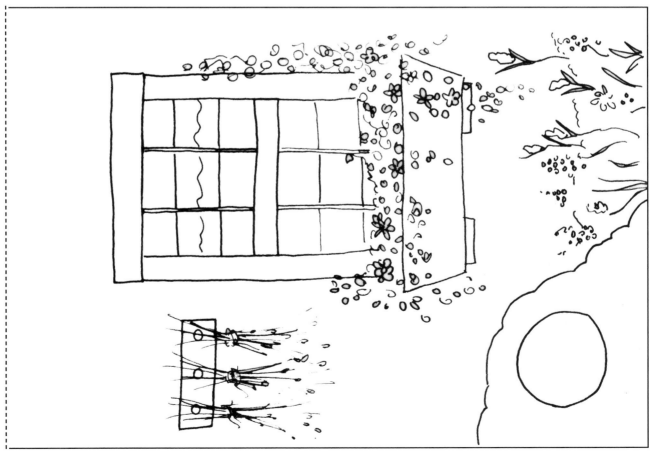

Pattern for side of Birdhouse

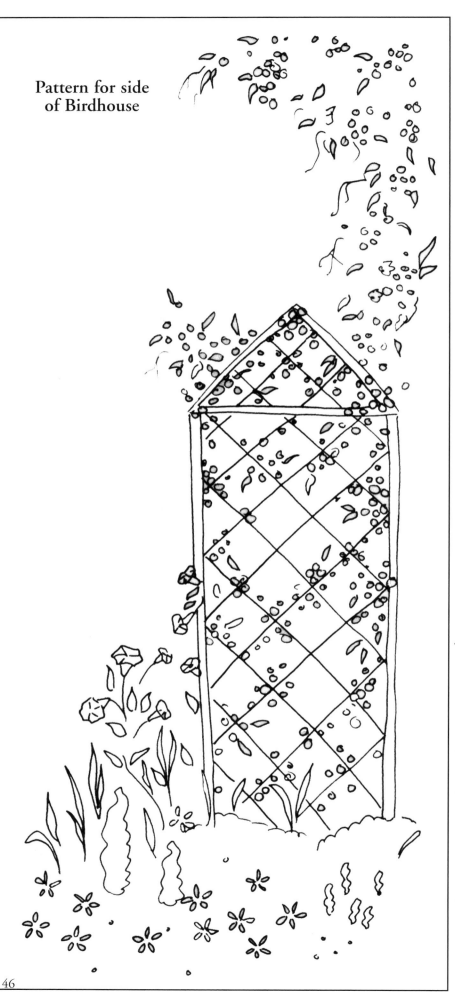

Sources

Acrylic Paints

Ceramcoat
Delta Technical Coatings
2550 Pellissier Place
Whittier, CA 90601
www.deltacrafts.com

Folk Art
Plaid Enterprises
3225 Westech Dr.
Norcross, GA 30092
www.plaidonline.com

Americana
DecoArt, Inc.
P.O. Box 386
Stanford, KY 40484
www.decoart.com

Brushes

Royal and Langnickel Brush Mfg., Inc.
6707 Broadway
Merrillville, IN 46410
219 660-4170

Sealer, Exterior/Interior Varnish, Metal Primer

Delta Technical Coatings

Dry-It Board

Winni Miller Dry-It Board
P.O. Box 3130
Fallbrook, CA 92088

Rusted Bucket, Shovel, and Pitchfork

Painting Goose
28780 Old Town Front St.
Temecula, CA 92590
www.thepaintinggoose.com

Produced by
Banar Designs, Inc.
P.O. Box 483
Fallbrook, CA 92088
banar@earthlink.net
www.banardesigns.com

Art Direction and Design: Barbara Finwall
Editorial Direction: Nancy Javier
Photography: Stephen Whalen
Photo Styling: Barbara Finwall
Computer Graphic Design: Wade Rollins
Computer Graphic Production: Chris Nelsen
Project Direction: Jerilyn Clements
Writing: Susan Borsch
Editing: Jerilyn Clements, Nancy Javier,
  Victoria Dye
Pattern Illustrations and Project Testing:
  Victoria Dye

PAINT CONVERSION CHART

Ceramcoat® by Delta	Americana™ by Decoart	Folk Art® by Plaid
Alpine Green 2439	Deep Teal	Tartan Green
Antique Gold 2002	Antique Gold	Yellow Ochre
Bahama Purple 2518	Wisteria	White+Periwinkle 3:1
Black Green 2116	Black Green	Wrought Iron
Blue Haze 2122	Blue Haze+White 1:1	Bluebell+Teal Green 2:1
Blue Heaven 2037	Baby Blue	Light Blue
Bridgeport Grey 2440	Slate Grey	Whipped Berry+Payne's Gray
Bungalow Blue 2575		Sterling Blue+Baby Blue (2:1)
Burnt Sienna 2030	Terra Cotta+Burnt Orange 1:1	Terra Cotta+Burnt Sienna 3:1
Burnt Umber 2025	Asphaltum	Burnt Sienna+Burnt Umber 1:1
Cactus Green 2463	Mint Julep+Jade 1:1	Poetry Green+White 3:1
Cape Cod Blue 2133	French Grey+Blue	Settler's Blue
Cayenne 2428	Delane's Dark Flesh	Cinnamon
Chamomile 2567	White+Yellow Ochre+Burnt Umber 2:1 (T)	French Vanilla+Camel 2:1
Charcoal 2436	Graphite	Charcoal Grey+Black 4:1
Chocolate Cherry 2538	Black Plum	Burnt Carmine
Dark Burnt Umber 2527	Burnt Umber	Burnt Umber+Burnt Sienna 2:1
Dark Foliage Green 2535	House Green Dark+Deep Teal 1:1	House Green Dark
Dark Forest Green 2096	Evergreen+Plantation Pine 1:1	Thicket
Dark Goldenrod 2519	Tangerine+Terra Cotta 2:1	Raw Sienna+Yellow Ochre 3:1
Deep Lilac 2577	Dioxazine Purple+(T) Cadmium Red	Violet Pansy
Dusty Mauve 2405	Cranberry Wine+Dioxazine Purple 3:1	Purple Passion
Eggplant 2486	Dioxazine Purple+True Red 2:1	Red Violet
Eggshell White 2539	White+Holly Green (T)	Spring White
Forest Green 2010	Avocado+Evergreen 2:1	Old Ivy
Fuchsia 2481	Royal Fuchsia	Magenta
Georgia Clay 2097	Burnt Orange (D)	Terra Cotta+Autumn Leaves 1:1
GP Purple 2091	Lavender+White 2:1	Lavender (D)
Hammered Iron 2094	Neutral Gray+Avocado (T)	Dapple Gray
Heritage Green 2494	Colonial Green+Sea Aqua 1:1	Mint Green+Tartan Green 1:1
Hippo Grey 2090	Neutral Grey	Medium Gray
Hydrangea Pink 2449	White+Spice Pink 3:1	White+Napthol Red Light 7:1
Lavender 2047	Lavender+Neutral Gray 3:1	Purple Lilac
Lavender Lace 2016	Flesh+Country Blue 3:1	Cotton Candy+Porcelain Blue 1:1
Lichen Grey 2118	Driftwood	Barn Wood
Lt. Foliage Green 2537	Hauser Light Green	Hauser Light Green
Light Ivory 2401	Light Buttermilk	Warm White
Lilac 2060	Orchid+Lavender 4:1	Amethyst
Magenta 2559	Red Violet	Fuchsia
Magnolia White 2487	White Wash	Wicker White
Medium Foliage Green 2536	Hauser Medium Green	Hauser Medium Green (AP)
Mello Yellow 2553	Taffy Cream+Moon Yellow 3:1	French Vanilla+Lemon Custard 8:1
Nightfall Blue 2131	Uniform Blue (L)	Denim Blue
Old Parchment 2092	Moon Yellow	Moon Yellow (Disc) or Sunflower+Buttercup 3:1
Opaque Red 2507	Calico Red	Christmas Red+Red Light 1:1
Pale Lilac 2576	Orchid+Lavender+White 4:l:l	Ballet Pink+Heather 4:1
Payne's Grey 2512	Payne's Grey	Payne's Grey+Prussian Blue (T)
Peachy Keen 2555	Flesh Tone+Medium Flesh 1:1	Skintone
Pink Quartz 2474	White+Raspberry 3:1	Raspberry Sherbet+White 1:1
Purple 2015	Dioxazine Purple	Purple
Purple Smoke 2548	Blue Violet + Violet Haze 3:1	Midnight+Lavender 3:1
Raw Linen 2546	Desert Sand	Clay Bisque (D)
Raw Sienna 2411	Raw Sienna	Yellow Light+Terra Cotta 2:1
Rosetta Pink 2430	Peaches N Cream+Dusty Rose (T)	Peach Perfection
Royal Fuchsia 2510	Royal Fuchsia+Plum 8:1	Fuchsia+Hot Pink 8:1
Rhythm 'N Blue 2551	Blue Violet+Dioxazine Purple 3:1	Brilliant Blue+Night Sky 4:1
Salem Blue 2121	Salem Blue	White+Azure Blue 4:1
Salem Green 2099	Teal Green+Cool Neutral 1:1	Teal Green+Blue Bonnet 2:1
Sandstone 2402	Desert Sand	Clay Bisque
Stonewedge Green 2442	Celery Green	Basil Green+Southern Pine 6:1
Straw 2078	Golden Straw	Buttercup
Tomato Spice 2098	Country Red	Red Light+Apple Spice 2:1
Vintage Wine 2434	Royal Purple	Dioxazine Purple+Heather 2:1
Wedgwood Green 2070	Jade Green	Bayberry
Wisteria 2467	Lavender+Cranberry Wine 3:1	Plumb Chiffon+White 2:1
Woodland Night Green 2100	Deep Teal	Wintergreen
White 2505	White (Snow or Titanium)	White (Titanium) (AP)

D - Dark   L - Light   T - Touch of   AP - Artists Pigment Color

MAKE EVERYTHING MORE BEAUTIFUL WITH DECORATIVE PANTING!

These books and other fine North Light titles are available from your local art & craft retailer, bookstore, online supplier or by calling 1-800-448-0915.

Add beauty and elegance to every room in your home! Diane Trierweiler makes it easy with step-by-step instructions for giving old furniture a facelift and new furniture a personal touch. You'll learn how to paint everything from berries to butterflies on chests, chairs and more. Includes 12 complete projects with color charts and traceable patterns.

ISBN 1-58180-234-X, paperback, 128 pages, #32009-K

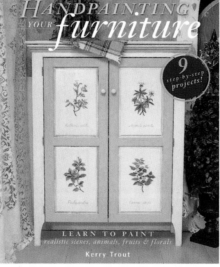

Transform your everyday outdoor furnishings into stunning, hand-painted garden accents. Acclaimed decorative painter Donna Dewberry shows you how to transform 15 deck, porch and patio pieces into truly lovely garden décor. Donna's easy-to-master brushwork techniques make each one fun and rewarding. No green thumb required!

ISBN 1-58180-144-0, paperback, 144 pages, #31889-K

You can turn an old or unfinished piece of furniture into a handpainted masterpiece! Kerry Trout provides 9 step-by-step projects that showcase an exciting array of realistic scenes and trompe l'oeil effects. Everything you need to know is inside, from preparing your surface to giving any piece an authentic, antique look.

ISBN 0-89134-980-4, paperback, 128 pages, #31539-K

Learn to paint miniature decorative painting masterpieces! These 14 full-color, step-by-step projects include everything from Victorian vanity boxes and wooden nesting dolls to holiday ornaments and more. Step-by-step instructions come with sidebars, materials lists, color palettes and designs ready to be hand-traced or photocopied.

ISBN 0-89134-992-8, paperback, 128 pages, #31541-K